The 14-Day Weight Loss Juicing Plan:

21 Quick, Delicious & Nutritious Juice Recipes To Jumpstart Your Weight Loss!

Ryan McNeal

Copyright © 2014

All Rights Reserved

[Click Here For Your Free Gift!](#)

Disclaimer

No part of this publication or the information in it may be quoted from or reproduced in any form by means such as printing, scanning, photocopying or otherwise without prior written permission of the copyright holder.

This publication is designed to provide accurate and personal information in regard to the subject matter covered. It is sold with the understanding that the publisher is not engaged in rendering medical, legal, or other professional service. If medical, legal, or other professional service is required, the services of a competent professional person should be sought.

Why I Wrote This Book

My name is Ryan McNeal. I've been actively involved in the health and wellness industry for many years. I know what works and what doesn't. What I'm going to share with you in the next couple of pages can literally transform your life..

You see, the health revolution is in full swing and in the middle of it all is the emphasis towards readily available, raw, unprocessed, and fresh foods - most notably fruits and vegetables.

Sadly though, one of the biggest hindrances for people to embrace the healthy revolution is their profound disgust – I think that's a bit too strong of a word although many would certainly argue that it's properly used in this context – for the taste of vegetables. Fruits don't suffer from the same level of rejection particularly because they're much easier on the taste buds… Although, it wouldn't take much to find people who actually prefer their meats and would rather avoid even the freshest vegetables and fruits.

Entering.. "The 14-Day Weight Loss Juicing Plan!" This is an honest attempt at making people realize that vegetables and fruits need not be bland, forgettable, or yucky.

Sure, cooking vegetables – particularly the green leafy ones – remains to be one of the classier and attractive options for enjoying veggies; but juicing, in reality, can offer just as much value – and actually more nutritional benefits – without the hassles and complications that come with having to learn how to become a master chef for all things healthy.

These are the very reasons why this ebook came to fruition. Like many people out there, I've long wanted to embrace the health revolution but the taste of vegetables, and fruits to a lesser degree, has always been a compelling reason for me to stay away. That was until I discovered that juicing solves many of the concerns that I have about enjoying fruits and vegetables.

To put it in simplest terms, juicing is easy and it allows me to enjoy fresh produce in all their glory after just a few minutes of fidgeting around in the kitchen. Juicing is great for people who want to be healthy but don't want to take the effort of becoming an expert in the kitchen (something that's not easy to do) nor have the patience to follow recipes from the internet or from the cookbook down to the last letter (also not an easy proposition for many).

This ebook is all about me sharing the simple joys of juicing along with the grand health benefits that can come from such a simple lifestyle change. So join me as I walk you through all that juicing has to offer. I can't promise that it would be as life-changing to you as it is to me; but I can tell you that juicing has the potential to turn your life around and point you in the right direction.

What awaits ahead is a fresh insight into how you can enjoy fruits and vegetables in a new and surprisingly simple manner, take in all the healthy benefits that juicing can offer, and ride the fresh wave of goodness towards your health and wellness goals.

I'm sure you'd be surprised that it can be "that" simple. I know I was when I first learned how to juice.

Now, Why Should You Read This Book?

Well, we all spend a good portion of our lives reading. In the morning, we read through newspapers and/or through our mobile devices to get an idea of what's happening around the world. More often than not, however, what we read is knowledge that gets filed in our brains never to be used again. And yet, you'd never consider your morning reading time as a waste.

This ebook provides knowledge that can help turn your life around, something that will come in handy if you are truly serious with your health and weight loss goals. The 14-Day Weight Loss Juicing Plan will give you 21 delightfully simple recipes that you can mix and match to suit your tastes and preferences with the simple goal of being able to lose weight after just 14 days.

These recipes are specifically chosen because they are simple to make but also because they take advantage of rather common ingredients that are often taken for granted by people like you and me.

Buy beyond that, the lessons in this weight loss juicing plan are also ideal stepping stones into a new, healthier and hopefully more permanent lifestyle that can help transform the way you live. Juicing everyday ingredients can be done in virtually any kitchen in the world and can help you detox, control your appetite, quench your thirst without the unnecessary calories, and give you a near endless supply of vitamins, minerals and antioxidants for a healthier and fitter body.

And that's just the beginning. The intention is to show you that juicing is so easy, you can virtually make your own recipes out of what is available in your area. And because it's healthy, weight loss becomes a natural consequence rather than a strict goal that you must aspire towards.

The idea that I'm trying to nurture here is that making simple choices – such as the ones available through juicing – can lead you to achieve your life's health goals. You don't need to make grand and complex promises in order to lose weight; oftentimes, the simplest choices yield the most powerful and transformative results.

So why should you take the time to read this ebook?

First, because it's a worthwhile endeavor to learn more about how to be healthier and fitter. And second, because you can be confident this is a reading exercise you are sure to appreciate for many more years afterwards. All that it takes is you spend the time to read.

If you are ready, then let's get the transformation started.

Table Of Contents

Disclaimer 2
Introduction 13
Powerful Health Benefits Of Juicing 17
    How Juicing Helps With Weight Loss 30
    Tips To Boost Your Juicing Experience 35
How To Store Your Fruits And Greens 37
    Refrigeration 38
    Freezing 41
    Countertop Storage 45
Choosing The Perfect Juicing Equipment 47
    Juicers vs. Blenders 49
    Different Types of Commercial Juicers 52
    Choosing The Best Juicer 56
Juicing 101: Make The Perfect Juice 61
    Making Juice with a Blender 63
    Making Juice With A Juicer 67
    Other Helpful Tips When Juicing 69
    Preparing Yourself For Juicing 71
Juicing Recipes For Weight Loss 75
    Perfect For The Morning 76

Green Goblet of Goodness 77
Ginger Ale 79
Beet and Apple Juice 81
A Juicy Jolt 83
Filler-Upper 85
Carrot Care 87
A Massive Green Breakfast 89

Afternoon Refreshments 91

Summertime Mojito 92
Energize Me! 94
Carrot-Mango Supreme 96
Tropicana Delight 98
Simple-and-Svelte Carrot and Apple Juice 100
Afternoon Surprise 102
Pick-Me-Up Delight 104

Perfect For Dinner 106

End-of-Day Ensemble 108
Weight Loss Watcher's Favorite 110
Grapefruits Galore 112
Cranberry Craziness 114
Sunset and Sexy 116
Sour-and-Sweet and Oh-So-Great 118
Extra-Veggie Extravaganza 120

The 14-Day Juicing Plan 122

How To Use This Plan 125

Conclusion 129

Introduction

Thank you for taking the time to sit down and begin this amazing journey towards your own personal health and wellness. You now stand on the precipice of what promises to be a turning point in the way you view and enjoy fruits and vegetables.

Today, it's very likely that you're only thinking of fruits and vegetables as bland options for snacks. It's also likely that you're one of those who assumes that the only good way to truly enjoy vegetables is to become really good a cooking.

Thankfully for people like me who are less than competent in the kitchen, juicing provides a convenient way out while still allowing me to enjoy fruits and veggies in a way that would make any nutritionist proud.

Along those very lines, this ebook promises to help you appreciate the power of juicing so you can take advantage of it to help turn your life around. Specifically, you should hope to learn the following simple but powerful lessons when juicing:

1. Identify which ingredients are suited to juicing. You'll quickly see from the recipes presented here that some ingredients appear more frequently than others because of their versatility and nutritive value.

2. Learn about the basics of juicing, from choosing the ingredients to preparing them, and then juicing them at home.

3. Know which equipment you need to buy. Do you need a blender or a juicer? Which type? At what cost?

4. Have a 14-day weight loss plan that you can use as basis for creating your own weight loss plan. A sample plan is well-and-good to get you started. A long-term plan for weight loss and embracing a healthier lifestyle requires that you learn the concepts and then apply them to suit your situation. That's how real and lasting lifestyle changes happen and this ebook should hopefully equip you with the knowledge to get you on the right track.

5. See for yourself that juicing does not need to be an exact science in order for you to reap the benefits. This is a truly transformative concept because it will allow you to understand that you can actually make your own recipes depending on your preferences.

The ebook is also laid out so you are being waked through the whole process from beginning to end. We'll begin by talking about the powerful health benefits of juicing to get you excited and amped up for what lies ahead. Then, we'll discuss the basics of what you need to know about juicing, the common and recurring ingredients, and important tips and tricks in storage.

From there, you'll find 21 different recipes organized into 3 sections – morning, afternoon and dinner-suitable juices.

All three sections touch on the three important aspects and benefits of juicing: weight loss, cleansing and detoxifying, and proper nutrition. Collectively, these aspects are intended to bring about a "brand new you" because all of these are essential in creating the transformation that you have always longed for from the inside out.

So, are you ready for the juicing revolution? If you are, then buckle up because we're now going to get the juices flowing and usher in the change that only a juiced lifestyle can deliver.

Powerful Health Benefits Of Juicing

Let's begin with the most obvious question: why is juicing suddenly becoming the next big trend in health and wellness? Is it really true or is juicing just another passing fad?

Well, people are attracted to juicing for a variety of reasons but here are the 10 most compelling and most common health benefits that people use to support their love for juicing.

1. It's A Great Way To Get Your Daily Dietary Requirement For Vitamins, Minerals And Antioxidants

Forget vitamin and mineral supplements from the pharmacy nearest you. Why would you want to take in something synthetic and artificial when fruits and vegetables refreshing can do the same job?

As it turns out, there is a compelling reason why vitamin and mineral supplements are necessary for many of us. Studies indicate that an average adult needs about 5 to 9 servings of fruits and vegetables per day in order to get our daily recommended dietary intake for vitamins and minerals. Sadly, most of us do not even reach half of this number for a variety of reasons.

Juicing is awesome because it helps "shortcut" the process so we can get our daily fix of recommended nutrients without having to chew our way through the 5 to 9 servings of fruit and vegetables per day.

Drinking a glass of orange juice is so much easier than having to eat 5 different mid-sized oranges so we can still have all the healthy goodness from fruits and vegetables without the platefuls that can quickly cause you to lose your appetite.

2. Juices Are Easier To Digest And Metabolize Than Solid Food

Liquids are easily absorbed through the stomach walls while solid food needs to be processed and broken down before the body can extract the nutrients inside.

In addition, the digestive process isn't fully-proof that you are guaranteed to extract all of the nutrients in the food that you eat. Chances are you end up extracting less than 100% of the nutrients in your food.

The nutrients from juices do not suffer from this problem. When dissolved in liquids, vitamins and minerals are already in a form that the body can handle quite easily. That means that you get your nutrients into your bloodstream faster than if you were to eat solid food.

3. All The Extra Nutrients From Juices Can Help Boost Your Immune System And Help Ward Off Unwanted Illnesses

One important, and often forgotten, reason for the increased prevalence of diseases is our inability to fuel our bodies with the right substances in the right amounts in order to equip it against foreign invaders.

The nutrition that you get in juices provide the nutrients that your body needs in order to be in peak condition so it doesn't become vulnerable to viruses and bacterial infection.

As a simple example, Vitamin C is one of the most powerful antioxidants known to man. Antioxidants are important in fighting diseases because it has the ability to react and neutralize foreign invaders before they can do damage. Increased intake of Vitamin C from citrus fruits can easily boost immunity and increase resistance against illnesses.

4. Aside From A Strengthened Immunity, There Are Many Other Health Benefits That Can Be Had With Fruit And Vegetable Juices

Proper nutrition can do wonders to your body. It will be able to work much more effectively and efficiently when nourished with the right nutrients. Your mood is better, you feel calmer and more peaceful, and you definitely feel less bloated and more able to take on your fair share of daily challenges.

Now, who wouldn't want to embrace those powerful health benefits to help you through a tough and challenging day?

5. Detoxification And Cleansing

Fruit and vegetables drinks are the best options if you want to detoxify and cleanse your body. Because it is in liquid form, it is able to wash away all the accumulated toxins from years of bad eating habits.

The fiber incorporated into blended juices sweep toxins from the intestinal tract. This works like the anti-clogging substance in your kitchen sink allowing for better digestion and a more "fluid" passage of food through the digestive system. A 3-day diet of nothing but fruit and vegetables juices is often a great way to kickstart a lifestyle change because it can quickly clean the body and prepare it for healthier food options moving forward.

In addition, green drinks, which belong to a special class of juices, are also considered alkalinizing foods. Alkalinizing foods are very important in cleansing diets because they can counteract the acidity of processed foods that we've been eating for so long. The acidic nature of processed foods destroys cells and damages your organs.

Counteracting this with a more alkaline diet will significantly help promote the health of your body beginning at the cellular level.

6. Weight Loss

Drinking more fruit and vegetable juices will allow you to move away from big portions of unhealthy processed foods that pack your body with empty calories.

Because juices are immensely nourishing, helping to satiate your body with all the good things that it needs, you are less likely to overeat or give in to your hunger pangs and food cravings. Adding juices to your daily diet will lead you to eat less without having to feel extremely hungry all the time.

In the next section, we will talk about weight loss and juicing in more detail so you'll have a better appreciation of how juicing can help you shed off those extra pounds.

7. Juicing Inadvertently Increases Your Fluid Intake

Improved understanding of the human body has led many doctors and medical professionals to believe that dehydration is an ever present problem for many. We lose fluids regardless of whether we are outside under the heat of the sun or in the comforts of our own offices, schools, or even inside our homes.

Juicing at least 3 times a day, can help mitigate and manage dehydration problems that you aren't aware were even there. Increased fluid intake also improves your kidney functions as it lowers your risk towards kidney stones and other kidney-related conditions like Urinary Tract Infection. In addition, proper hydration can also help address minor but annoying medical conditions like dehydration-induced headaches.

Think about dehydration the next time you grab a drink and ask yourself if what you're holding can actually be better than a glass of freshly-squeezed fruit.

8. Getting Your Protein Source From Non-Animal Sources

Variation is a key component in any balanced diet and getting your protein from non-animal sources is no exception. While plants do not have as much protein as animal products do, you can be confident that you are getting protein without the side effects that come with meat products – fats and unhealthy fatty acids, uric acid, and cholesterol, to name a few.

To boost your protein intake while continuing to enjoy your juices, you only need to add some specially chosen ingredients to your drinks juice to bring its protein content up to par with most meat-heavy diets.

For example, simple tweaks like adding nuts such as baked peanuts or almonds, as well as cooked quinoa and other whole grains can already help in diversifying your protein sources to include plant-based proteins.

9. Healthy Sugars

In today's calorie-crazed culture, "healthy sugars" may sound like an oxymoron but it is actually one of the most important aspects of a healthy and balanced diet.

Not surprisingly, the most important source of healthy sugars are fruits and vegetables which have natural sugars like fructose that carry a myriad of health benefits without the consequence of increased calorie intake.

For one, the body metabolizes natural sugars differently than it would with commercial sweeteners. We already known of common table sugar and many of us use it regularly to flavor our coffee and other drinks. Sucrose is a complex sugar that contains glucose and fructose bound together. It's fattening because when it is digestive, the glucose immediately goes into the bloodstream and can eventually be metabolized into fat that is then deposited in your arms, thighs, mid-section and around the internal organs.

Fructose, on the other hand, is a simple sugar which requires some additional metabolic steps before it can be used by the body. Those additional metabolic steps burn energy so your net energy gain is lower than with sucrose. In addition, the metabolic processes that convert fructose to the usable glucose form also takes time so the sugar doesn't immediately go into your bloodstream to become fat.

The science may be complicated but it highlights a simple idea, some sugars are better than others. Where you get your sugar makes a lot of difference towards whether or not you put on additional weight.

10. Pound-For-Pound, The Most Nutritious Meal You Can Have In A Day Is The One That Comes In The Form Of A Drink.

Fruit and vegetable juices are highly versatile because you can pick almost any ingredient in order to have the type of nutrients you want in your juice.

You can alternate between different types of vegetables and fruits to get a varied package of vitamins, minerals, enzymes, antioxidants, and phytochemicals all in one day. You cannot say the same for other types of diet which are almost always based on one major ingredient and contains a limited number of healthy substances.

How Juicing Helps With Weight Loss

Now, of all the health benefits that we talked about, it wouldn't be a far reach to say that "weight loss" got your attention the most. Recent studies indicate that weight is becoming a serious issue in many countries across the world.

In the US, for example, a 2010 survey by the National Center for Health Statistics indicate that as many as 35% of American adults already fall into the "obese" classification. That means that as many as 90 million Americans now have a growing problem with excess weight.

The situation isn't any better in many other industrialized countries. A recent story from the International Business Times lists Mexico, Australia, New Zealand, United Kingdom, Canada, Ireland, Chile, Iceland and Hungary as the other 9 countries that collectively make up the list of the Top10 Most Obese Countries in the World.

A United Nations study also supported these statistics and it even indicates that as many as 70% of Mexicans are now categorically overweight and as many as 33% of Mexican teenagers are also facing weight problems at a very young age.

Certainly, poor food choices and work habits that promote a sedentary lifestyle are to blame. The convenience offered by fast food in industrialized countries undoubtedly plays a massive role in this catastrophe. However, the core of the issue isn't that more and more McDonalds are available in street corners around the world. It is that people nowadays no longer have the knowledge that allows them to make correct decisions about what to eat.

If somebody were to ask you what constitutes as a healthy diet, what would you say?

There's a very good chance you'll be able to give an answer that alludes to increase consumption of food and vegetables; and that's correct. But there's a more pressing and difficult question that comes after that.

Just how can you teach someone, anyone really, to enjoy fruits and vegetables on a daily basis? If you're not a chef, just as I am not, then thinking of "healthy recipes" that use more fruits and vegetables and minimizes fried foods can be a very daunting and horrifying adventure.

This is where juicing becomes a very powerful tool for weight loss.

We've already touched the reasons why juicing is important towards losing weight and here we list them again for emphasis.

    A. Juicing helps control your appetite. Because your body is equipped with a more balanced set of nutrients, you are more likely to crave less and in the process avoid unhealthy food options.

B. Juicing gives you healthy sugars. Natural sugars make you feel full without the extra calories.

If you want to lose weight from juicing as this 14-day plan suggests, you have to embrace these benefits and build on them as you sustain your newfound lifestyle. The most successful weight loss journeys are the ones that can be sustained over a longer period.

You can expect juicing to steer you in the right direction but if you don't embrace the change and eventually revert back told habits, you can never expect to make the weight loss permanent.

The 14-day plan in the outlined here will be a very helpful guide but it won't make you achieve the results on their own. You have to commit to the desire to change and have the fortitude to stick with it. Juicing will somewhat make it easier but you have to remember that no weight loss journey is ever truly easy. If you can grasp that concept, then you are already halfway towards reaping the results that you want.

Now, just what do you need to do to learn how to juice?

Tips To Boost Your Juicing Experience

Smoothies, fruit shakes, fruit juices, green cocktails... When people are asked about what they think healthy drinks are, those choices are the ones that often come to mind. No wonder, supermarket shelves the world over are flooded with all sorts of commercial brands of pre-packaged, industrially prepared and artificially sweetened fruit shakes and fruit juices all designed to appeal to your preconceived notions of what it means to be healthy.

This ebook on juicing appeals to the same idea but with one obvious and glaring difference: you are juicing your own drink and not pouring from a plastic bottle so you know exactly what goes into every sip. Do you want sugar or do you choose to flavor it with honey instead?

A home-made green shake only has the ingredients that you want; it does not hide anything or contain anything that you can't pronounce or spell. No artificial ingredients, no artificial sweeteners, no preservatives, no artificial flavoring – that is juicing at its purest, absolute and "most effective" best, and that's where the results flow from.

It's that simple! And it inevitably starts when you buy your fruits and greens and decide how to best store them.

How To Store Your Fruits And Greens

There are three common options for storing fruits and greens in the home. Each of these options has its own set of pros and cons, most notably that certain fruits and vegetables are compatible with one storage method but not with another.

The goal is to select the right method for storing your ingredients so you can be assured that they'll last longer, will retain their nutritive value, and will remain as fresh as the day you first bought them at the supermarket.

The options we will talk about are refrigeration, freezing, and countertop storage.

Refrigeration

Firstly, it is very important to draw the line between refrigeration and freezing here. Technically, refrigeration means you are bringing the temperature to just above zero and not lower. This means that the water in the fruits and veggies remain liquid and are not really "frozen."

Contrast this with freezing where the storage temperature is brought down to below freezing. We've already mentioned how both these alternatives have their fair share of pros and cons and we'll talk about freezing in more detail in the next section.

So, back to refrigeration... Most fruits and vegetables are very compatible with refrigeration particularly when placed in the crisper. The "just above" freezing conditions lock the moisture in the leaves or the skin allowing them to remain fresher for longer periods.

A study by Cornell University in the US classifies these conditions as "cool and moist" storage conditions and provides a short list of recommended fruits and vegetables that thrive in these conditions.

Table 1. Fruits And Vegetables That Require Cool, Moist Conditions (Refrigeration).

Vegetable	Temperature (°F)	Relative Humidity (%)	Length of Storage
Beans, snap	40-50	95	7-10 days
Cucumbers	45-50	95	10-14 days
Eggplant	45-50	90	1 week
Cantaloupe	40	90	15 days
Watermelon	40-50	80-85	2-3 weeks
Peppers, sweet	45-50	95	2-3 weeks
Potatoes, early	50	90	1-3 weeks
Potatoes, late	40	90	4-9 months
Tomatoes, green	50-70	90	1-3 weeks
Tomatoes, ripe	45-50	90	4-7 days

In addition, please remember that vegetables and fruits do don't take well to refrigeration should not be stored in the same compartment as leafy vegetables and vice versa. The most common examples are peppers and pumpkins. These fruits and vegetables decay quickly in cool and moist conditions and in the process they emit gases that promote the decay of green leaves.

However, if you have no other choice but to combine these fruits and vegetables together in one crisper, try using plastic bags to isolate the green leaves. This reduces their exposure to the other vegetables in the crisper and could help prolong the storage life by another day or two.

As a general rule, different vegetables have a different refrigerator life depending on its nature and on the actual storage conditions. Make sure to familiarize yourself with the tendencies of your preferred ingredients so you know how soon you need to juice these vegetables before they lose their freshness and crispiness.

Freezing

Most fruits and leafy greens are actually perfect for freezing provided you know what to do in order to lock in the nutrients and the moisture. The table below provides a very extensive of ingredients that thrive in cold and moist storage.

However, immediately freezing the vegetables without any prior preparation can damage the plant cells resulting in that familiar "black goo" you see at the bottom of the crisper or any other refrigerator compartment.

Thankfully, it's not difficult to learn how to prepare your juicing ingredients for frozen storage. Clean the fruits and greens first to make sure there are no unwanted soil particulates or extra hard stems that do not freeze well and can initiate the rotting process.

For leafy vegetables, a few extra steps are required but if you learn to master the following steps, then your frozen storage would be a heaven for your juicing needs:

1. Blanch briefly to stop the work of enzymes that promote the decay of plant leaves. When done properly, blanching will help give your greens that bright color and great flavor after being frozen for a few days. The right way is to dip the greens into a pot of boiling water very quickly. Make sure you don't prolong the process or the vegetables will cook and you'll have nothing left for a fresh green smoothie days after.

2. Drain the hot water and wash the vegetables in cold water to immediately stop the cooking process.

3. Make sure there are no water accumulations in the leaves right before freezing. For this, squeeze the leaves hard so you extract the

water out leaving only a compressed ball of greens that are ready for freezing.

4. Chop the greens before storage. You are eventually going to juice or cook them so chopping them at this stage makes little difference to the final product. Besides, chopping increases the surface area of the greens ensuring that all trapped water is squeezed out before freezing.

5. Bag and label before putting in the freezer.

Table 2. Fruits And Vegetables That Require Cold, Moist Conditions (Freezing).

Vegetable	Temperature (°F)	Relative Humidity (%)	Length of Storage
Asparagus	32-36	95	2-3 weeks
Apples	32	90	2-6 months
Beets	32	95	3-5 months
Broccoli	32	95	10-14 days
Brussels Sprouts	32	95	3-5 weeks
Cabbage, Early	32	95	3-6 weeks
Cabbage, Late	32	95	3-4 months
Cabbage, Chinese	32	95	1-2 months
Carrots, mature	32	95	4-5 months
Carrots, immature	32	95	4-6 weeks
Cauliflower	32	95	2-4 weeks
Celeriac	32	95	3-4 months
Celery	32	95	2-3 months
Collards	32	95	10-14 days
Corn, sweet	32	95	4-8 days
Endive, Escarole	32	95	2-3 weeks
Grapes	32	90	4-6 weeks
Kale	32	95	10-14 days
Leeks, green	32	95	1-3 months
Lettuce	32	95	2-3 weeks
Parsley	32	95	1-2 months
Parsnips	32	95	2-6 months
Pears	32	95	2-7 months
Peas, green	32	95	1-3 weeks
Potatoes, early	50	90	1-3 weeks
Potatoes, late	39	90	4-9 months
Radishes, spring	32	95	3-4 weeks
Radishes, winter	32	95	2-4 months
Rhubarb	32	95	2-4 weeks
Rutabagas	32	95	2-4 months
Spinach	32	95	10-14 days

Freezing allows fruits and vegetables to last for quite a long time, up to a few months in some cases, as long as they don't thaw and freeze repeatedly. Remember this the next time you pack vegetables into storage so juicing ingredients don't overstay their welcome in your freezer.

Countertop Storage

For leafy greens, the countertop is often the most hostile environment for storage particularly when you are living in a hot and humid area and the air-conditioning isn't turned on the whole time. Leaves can quickly dehydrate and wither and with it, all hope of a fresh green juice is gone into thin air. With the A/C on, green leafy vegetables stand a much better chance of surviving for a day or two although as a general rule, it is not really advisable to store them on the countertop.

For fruits, however, the countertop can be much more accommodating especially for those that have thicker skin which prevents moisture from escaping into the atmosphere thereby preserving the fruit or vegetable for a longer period.

Table 3. Fruits And Vegetables That Require Cool, Dry Conditions.

Vegetable	Temperature (°F)	Relative Humidity (%)	Length of Storage
Garlic	32	65-70	6-7 months
Onions	32	65-70	6-7 months

Table 4. Fruits And Vegetables That Require Warm, Dry Conditions.

Vegetable	Temperature (°F)	Relative Humidity (%)	Length of Storage
Peppers, hot	50	60-65	6 months
Pumpkins	50-55	70-75	2-3 months
Squash, winter	50-55	50-60	2-6 months
Sweet Potato	55-60	80-85	4-6 months

When it doubt, you can quickly run an online search for a specific fruit or vegetable that you want to store so you can find out whether that ingredient will last longer in the refrigerator, in the freezer or on the countertop.

Choosing The Perfect Juicing Equipment

After storage, you can now begin thinking about juicing your ingredients. For this, the juicer is your most dependable weapon towards producing spectacular and thirst-quenching drinks every time. As such, you should spend some time researching about the perfect juicer before you decide what brand or model you should buy from your local supermarket.

Now, here's a word of caution on buying juicers: make sure you don't go to the store without knowing anything about juicers and/or blenders. You will only be swayed by marketing techniques that are designed to make you close the sale even if you end up with a product that doesn't suit your needs.

The first thing you need to know is whether you want to get a juicer or a blender. Yes, those two are very different from each other and your choice dictates the types of ingredients that you can use and the type of drink that you produce.

So here are the basics.

Juicers vs. Blenders: Which One Should You Get?

Juicers extract the juice out of fruits and vegetables and as a result, you get pure juice with relatively low fiber content. In contrast, blenders produce smoothies where the ingredients are all blended together producing thick shakes. In the case of green ingredients, many often associate this smoothie with that "yucky" taste because you get everything blended into the drink, leaves and stems included.

Of course, it all boils down to preference. More specifically, would you rather have a high fiber drink or a pure juice? Both have roughly the same nutrition value if the ingredients are the same except that with smoothies, your digestive tract is put through more work – and may also reap more substantial cleansing rewards – than with juiced options.

Beyond that, there are other more tangible differences which give rise to different benefits. For example, smoothies from blenders tend to store better in the refrigerator than juices. The fiber in smoothies also help regulate the rate of sugar absorption by the intestinal walls so you don't go through the sugar spikes and sugar crashes that are very common with sweetened drinks. Blenders also tend to be more versatile as a kitchen appliance so if you are looking for a go-to workhorse that can also be used for preparing salsa and sauces, the blender is your best bet because juicers almost always only do one thing: juice!

On the flipside, juicers also have their fair share of advantages. First, juices are readily absorbable by the digestive tract so you get all the nutrients in an instant. That also means an instantaneous energy boost, if you ever need one. Second, juicers can handle almost any produce while blenders are often limited to softer fruits and vegetables that can be "mashed" by the spinning blender blades. This is why it's much easier to juice a carrot than it is to blend it. That versatility significantly cuts into the time you need to prepare for juicing a pile of ingredients versus blending them.

In the end, it's not easy recommending one over the other if you don't know how you intend to use them. The easy answer is to say that both are comparable and deliver just about the same nutritive value so arguing about which one is better almost becomes a moot point.

Perhaps the most compelling determinant is your preference for smoothies or for juices; do you like one over the other? If you are, then you should already have an idea whether a juicer or a blender works best for you.

For purposes of this ebook, we will focus on juicers primarily because "juicing" is more frequently associated to juices – yes, it is that simple really, but also because the "juiced" versions don't have the perceived "yuck" of thick blended smoothies.

Different Types of Commercial Juicers

Consumers don't often bother with the exact type but if you are the technically inclined, you will end up appreciating this section.

In general, there are 5 types of juicers on the market each with its own pros and cons.

1. **Centrifugal Juicers.** These are the most common varieties on the market and have the characteristic upright cylindrical shape. The mechanism is also simple: the fruits are sliced (or grated) into tiny bits before pressed through a sieve to separate the juices. These also tend to work faster and have larger feeding sections so bigger chunks of vegetables and fruits can be juiced together at once. The only downside with centrifugal juicers is that these do not tend to work well with green leafy ingredients because the stringy leaves are harder to

squeeze through the juicing blade. Click here for the best centrifugal juicers

2. **Masticating Juicers.** The name itself is a dead giveaway; the juicer works by "chewing" the ingredients in a combination of grinding and crushing action. These work well with leafy greens and are also known to be more durable than most other types. The downside is that the cutting action requires a smaller feeding section so you are forced to do more work to get the same volume of juice. The slightly higher cost is also not doing anyone any favors. Click here for the best masticating juicers

3. **Wheatgrass Juicers.** As the name implies, this is specifically designed for juicing wheatgrass. As you can see, the application is fairly limited although if you are into wheatgrass juices, investing in this type of

juicer is beyond any doubt a necessity. [Click here for the best wheatgrass juicers](#)

4. **Triturating Juicers.** These are high-end juicers that are often also priced accordingly. They function much like masticating juicers but are specifically controlled so that the "chewing" action preserves as much of the nutrients. This leads to a slightly more complex operation that may become a concern for most users in terms of maintenance and repair cost. In general, the purchase and operations cost are big concerns for health enthusiasts on a budget. But is a great investment towards your health, if it fits within your budget. [Click here for the best triturating juicers](#)

5. **Citrus Juicers.** These juicers are specifically designed for extracting juice from citrus fruits. Unfortunately, the design elements make these juicers ill-suited for making juice from leafy vegetable ingredients. This is another thing you

need to be aware lest you end up with a juicer that doesn't help you make green juices. [Click here for the best citrus juicers](#)

Choosing The Best Juicer

What is the definition of the perfect juicer? That is one tough question that may not have a universal answer. You can, however, refer to some general guidelines that can help you narrow down your selection.

1. **How Often Do You Plan To Use Your Juicer?** Frequent, heavy-duty use requires better quality juicers if you want yours to last long enough. You may be forced to pay for top dollar to get the most reliable model in the market but if you are determined to "squeeze" every last ounce of performance from your juicer because you depend on it on a daily basis, then quality becomes your most important consideration regardless of cost.

2. **How Fast Does The Juicer Work?** Juicing typically does not require a long time but some low-end juicer designs with smaller feeding mouths can prolong the process unnecessarily. If you often drink your juice in the morning right before work and you have to catch the train or

bus shortly after, a faster working juicer can be a worthwhile investment.

3. **How Noisy Is A Particular Brand When Juicing?** This is a tricky question to answer. How noisy is too noisy? Most juicers have been tested to comply with consumer regulations on noise level so it would be foolish to expect a significant difference between two models of varying price points. Still, you might want to test out your preferred juicers at the store so you know just how much noise you are signing up for by buying a specific model.

4. **What Ingredients Work With What Juicer Brands?** We've already covered this when we talked about the types of juicers. For newbies to juicing, having a preference outright cannot be expected until you've tried to make a few juices or smoothies on your own. If you want to juice fibrous veggies, common centrifugal juicers should be okay but if you

prefer more greens than fruits, you might want to consider getting triturating juicers.

So, which is the best juicer on the market? Here are general guidelines that should help narrow down your options:

1. **Low-End Option: The Ordinary Countertop Juicer.** These are the types that cost about $100 to $150 and are readily available in almost any store across the country and the world over. This can be a great entry juicer that should last you a couple of years. If you are not yet sure about your juicing habits, start-out with this type and then upgrade later on if you decide that you want a more reliable and higher-end model.

2. **Mid-Level Option: The Omega Series.** There are various models starting with the 8005 and 8006 which costs about $220 to $280. These juicers are already able to handle greens quite

effectively at a lower price point than what the Green Star offers. If you are on a budget, you can invest in an Omega and should have no problem squeezing out your juices from most types of ingredients.

3. **High-End Option: The Green Star.** This is a top-of-the-line model costing about $450 and higher depending on the specific make and specifications. Only buy the Green Star if you are a serious juicer and you want a triturating type juicer ready and available at any time of the day for any ingredient that you want to juice.

Just to cover our bases, it's worthwhile to leave a few words about blenders.

If you are a big fan of smoothies more than juices and are out looking for a good blender, you cannot go wrong with Vitamix although there are also a number of models and brands to choose from of comparable make and specification. Also, you can consider the same basic considerations for juicers as these also hold true for most blenders.

In the end, take the time to think your choice through by considering your planned usage, the price, and the dependability of the resulting product before making the purchase.

Juicing 101: Make The Perfect Juice

Juicing is actually very easy to do.

All that you need is your trusted juicer, a few choice selections of the best ingredients, and you are set. The one thing to remember, and I cannot emphasize this hard enough, is that juicing is a matter of personal preference so you have all the control in the world in deciding what goes into every drink.

Of course, it doesn't hurt to follow a few recipes to learn firsthand how certain ingredients work with others – and you'll have 21 samples to choose from in the latter section. Once you get a feel for what works and what doesn't, you can quickly make decisions on how to go about making your juice.

In a nutshell, here's how you can juice or blend depending on what equipment you have and what you intend to make: a smoothie or a juice.

Making Juice with a Blender

We've already covered how blenders are specifically designed to make smoothies because you don't separate the fiber from the juice. When using a blender, therefore, expect a thicker consistency of the resulting drink. The one on the left is a berry smoothie or shake while the picture on the right is on an orange juice from a countertop juicer.

To begin making the juice, gather together all the ingredients that you intend to use. Cut them into smaller chunks so they can be effectively mashed or chopped by your blender. A good rule of thumb is to cut the ingredients into 1-cm size cubes that are easily blended together into a smoothie.

Aside from the regular ingredients, it is also common practice to add a cup of water or ice cubes to the blend. This helps to ensure that the blade doesn't stick as well as provide a medium where the mashed up ingredients can all come together. If you want, you can also substitute water with fruit juices or milk so you end up with something different each and every time you blend.

However, if you intend to use bottled or pre-packaged fruit juices to "spice up" your smoothie, always remember to check the label so you know the sugar and other additives that go into your drink.

Another important consideration for blenders is that you have control as to how long you want to "pulse" the ingredients together to get the quality that you want. Longer pulsing will produce a more homogenous mixture while shorter pulses may leave behind bigger chunks of fruits and vegetables.

As a rule, high-end blenders tend to be more powerful and are able to do more work – chopping, mashing and blending – during a shorter time period. You need to be familiar with your blender to know how long it will normally take to mash the ingredients together but this is generally not a difficult task since you can taste as you go during the blending process.

You can also produce pure juice out of a resulting smoothie by using a sieve to filter the fiber from the juice. The smaller the sieve size, the better is the separation that you will get. You can also use a spoon to press on the pulp on top of the sieve to make sure all the liquid is extracted. If you don't do this, there's a very good chance you only end up with half a glass of green juice and majority of the nutrients are separated with the fiber and the remaining liquid and thrown into waste.

Once you finish filtering the juice, you now have a drink that you can enjoy for both its refreshing and nutritious qualities.

Making Juice With A Juicer

This is often much easier than when using a blender.

After you've prepared your ingredients, check to see if the sizes fit into the feeding mouth of the juicer. If not, cut the fruits and veggies accordingly to fit.

Simply start the juicer as indicated in the manufacturer's manual and ensure that cup is placed in the discharge before you start juicing the ingredients.

When everything is in place, put in the ingredients into the feeder section and using the pusher, push the ingredients into the chamber. Do this for all the ingredients on your plate. Wait for the last drops of juice to come out before you get the cup from the discharge.

And that's it! You now have a juice that packs a lot of health benefits and only took 5 minutes to make!

Other Helpful Tips When Juicing

You can also take note of the following tips to bring extra pizzazz to your juicing experience:

1. Combine different varieties of ingredients. For example, leafy greens like kale and spinach and alkaline veggies like cucumber and broccoli work well together with a naturally sweet fruit like mango or banana. By experimenting with different ingredients together, you are expanding the nutritional value of the drink and also improving the taste by virtue of the different ingredients complementing each other and no single ingredient overpowering all the others.

2. Be liberal with your fruit selections but think of fruits that are in season as these tend to be cheaper. Green apples and pears, for example, are widely common but depending on where you are in the world, mango can become a problem especially in the winter months. Scout your local grocers for cheap fresh ingredients.

Juicing need not be an expensive venture if you how to mix and match your ingredients depending on the time of year.

3. Add some spice. Grated ginger provides a subtle kick but you can also experiment with a few other selections like paprika, cumin, or even a pinch of chili powder if you are a bit daring. When it comes to flavoring juices, your imagination is really the limit.

4. For relatively sweet juices like those made from apples and pears or green juices from spinach and kale, you can always squeeze a lemon on top for some added flair and some much needed acidity.

5. If you must sweeten the drink, use honey. Stay away from refined sugars and other commercial sweeteners that can ruin your diet plan.

Preparing Yourself For Juicing

While juicing is quite easy to do and can be done by anyone, it should not be taken lightly. By this I mean that no one should attempt to just switch to drinking juices because they want to lose weight and be healthier. Like all things related to becoming healthier, there's a right way and a wrong way to juice and being prepared before juicing is an important component of doing things the right way.

Before you start to juice and shift your diet accordingly, here are some serious considerations that you should take time to think through.

1. **How Is Your Current Health Level?** Not everyone can start juicing outright. Diabetics, for example, will have problems with green juices that have high-sugar content because the sugar spike can trigger an attack.

    The recommendation here is to check for any medical flags that may prevent you from juicing. Are you allergic to certain ingredients like nuts? Do you have hyperacidity which can be worsened by certain ingredients such as citrus fruits?

Talk to your doctor about your current health and be open about your plans for juicing so you can prepare accordingly before you start with a program similar to this 14-day weight loss juicing plan.

2. **Are You Ready For The Changes That Will Happen Once You Start Juicing?** A common example is having withdrawal symptoms the moment one switches to green juices instead of coffee or tea. Headaches are common temporary side effects that need to be managed in the interim.

You need to be ready for changes like this so you are not caught off-guard as you transition into a healthier diet and lifestyle. Often, people fail in their quest to become permanent juicers because they weren't able to overcome the hurdles of withdrawal syndrome.

Weakness, rashes, muscle soreness, loss of focus… these are just some of the symptoms that one is likely to experience during the initial stages of switching from one substance to green drinks and physical and mental preparation are integral towards eventual success.

As a point of emphasis, remember that juicing is intended to bring you into a refreshed lifestyle, one that is free from the old habits that fueled your unhealthy choices. That decision will never be easy, but it can be managed.

Your challenge is to make sure you are ready to take on the demands of the new lifestyle so you can assure yourself of success instead of eventually reverting back to old habits and allowing your body to relapse into its vicious and health-damaging tendencies.

Juicing Recipes For Weight Loss

The juicing recipes that follow are subdivided into three sections, namely those that are perfect for the morning, those that work well with afternoon and snacks, and then those that are perfect for dinner.

Of course, the reality is that these juices and smoothies are actually highly interchangeable and can be drunk at any time during the day.

However, there are certain elements to these drinks that make them better suited as morning starters or dinner accompaniment so we will take advantage of those characteristics to match the drink to the your meals.

Perfect For The Morning

Everyone has a different idea about what constitutes the perfect breakfast. Some want their breakfast as light as possible while others prefer heavier meals to get them going through the day.

Whatever your preference may be, these 7 juices and smoothies are specifically designed to get your day started in the best way possible: by being healthy and mindful of your pursuit of losing weight in a sustainable and efficient manner.

Green Goblet of Goodness

Serving Size: 6-7 ounces

Best Prepared With: Centrifugal or Masticating Juicers

You will find apples a recurring ingredient in many of these drinks. Studies have shown that apples lead to more weight loss in people who are dieting or juicing than if the same people weren't incorporating apples into their daily diets.

The reasons behind this is not yet clearly understood but researchers seem to think it is the fructose in apples combined with the high levels of antioxidants that are worthy of the credit.

So if you are looking for major results from juicing, this green goblet of goodness is just the thing to set you in the right direction.

Ingredients:

4 medium apples (about 720 grams)

3 stalks of celery

2 leaves of kale

1 medium lemon, peeled

4 cups of spinach

Directions:

1. Process all ingredients in a juicer, shake or stir and serve.

Ginger Ale

Serving Size: 6-7 ounces

Best Prepared With: Centrifugal Juicers

The hero of the recipe is clearly the ginger as it provides a kick that elevates the taste of the apples, celery and cucumber. The addition of the lime also adds some much needed acidity to complement the ginger.

In terms of actual health benefits, the ginger also brings its fair share of goodness to the show. Ginger is a warming herb and is actually well known as a fever buster. When consumed regularly, ginger can facilitate improved blood flow which can help cleanse the blood from toxins as well as lower blood pressure and prevent the formation of clots which can lead to other sorts of illnesses.

The addition of ginger in this "ale" recipe also highlights one important thing with juicing; just a few minor tweaks in your ingredients already produces vastly different results in terms of nutritional and health benefits. You would do extremely well to experiment in the kitchen using common and readily available ingredients that can significantly boost your health.

Ingredients:

3 medium apples (about 550 grams)

2 stalks of celery

1 medium cucumber

1 thumb of ginger (about 20 grams)

1 lime

Directions:

1. If you are new to juicing, it is best that you peel and grate the ginger using a standard cheese grater. This will allow it to be better integrated into the juice. You should also peel the lime if you are not yet familiar with the bitter taste of lime skin.
2. Juice everything and enjoy!

Beet and Apple Juice

Serving Size: 3-4 ounces
Best Prepared With: Centrifugal Juicers

You already know about apples but do you know that beets are also antioxidant-rich and ideal for weight loss? Red beets contain betalains which have natural anti-inflammatory properties and are important for helping you to detoxify. Embrace this apple and beet juice concoction and add it to your morning ritual for a heavy, filling, but healthy dimension to weight loss juicing routine.

Ingredients:

1 small beet, chopped
4 medium-sized carrots, peeled chopped
1 medium apple, cored, chopped
¼ cup fresh mint sprigs

Directions:

1. Juice the beet, then carrots, then the apple in that order. Juice the mint sprigs last and make sure to stir before drinking.

A Juicy Jolt

Serving Size: 4-5 ounces

Best Prepared With: Centrifugal or Masticating Juicers

If you're like me and you hate waking up every early in the morning, you know that a cup of coffee can often be the difference-maker between a rather drab commute to work and a fantastic start to your day. Now, imagine substituting your coffee with this juicy jolt of healthy goodness.

The secret to the juicy jolt's success is its balanced approach to nutrition. As such, you can skip breakfast without worrying about hunger pangs. The apples and cucumber provide volume and heft to your liquid meal while the lemon and orange give it that tangy taste that makes everyone pine for a glass of freshly-squeezed orange juice.

No doubt you'll also love this simple but fulfilling juice to get your morning started.

Ingredients:

2 medium apples, cored

1 medium orange

1 small cucumber

¼ lemon, peeled

3 kale leaves

Directions:

1. Juice everything together and enjoy.

Filler-Upper

Serving Size: 3-4 ounces

Best Prepared With: Centrifugal Juicers

Like the juicy jolt, this juicing recipe is useful if you want to completely do away with breakfast without having to deal with the hunger pangs that come around mid-morning. The answer to that, as usual, are apples and cucumber. This particularly recipe, however, goes another extra mile by introducing you to the idea of adding protein powder to your drinks.

Protein powders are tricky because there are many different brands on the market and you actually never know which ones are okay. Still, if you are able to find the right brand, a protein powder is an excellent complement to a juicing recipe because it adds protein into your drink, a fantastic substitute for a largely meatless diet plan.

Without specifically advocating for a specific protein powder brand, you should be able to find good products from known brands like Whey and Cellucor among others.

Ingredients:

1 small cucumber

3 stalks of celery, leaves included

1 medium apple, cored

2 tablespoons of protein powder

Directions:

1. Juice the cucumber, celery and apple as you would in any other recipe.
2. Stir the protein powder into the juice.
3. Enjoy!

Carrot Care

Serving Size: 5-6 ounces

Best Prepared With: Masticating or Triturating Juicers

Next to apples, carrots are probably the most well-known of healthy ingredients. Bugs Bunny surely had a part to play in that but the well-known properties of the carrot can already make this Carrot Care recipe a definite sell.

Carrots are rich in an antioxidant known as beta carotene which is a precursor for the formation of Vitamins A and C. Regular consumption of carrots, therefore, help boost immunity as well as improve vision.

The fiber in carrots also play a crucial role in detoxifying diets and this can be instrumental for people who are eyeing a better number on the bathroom weight scale.

Ingredients:

4 large carrots

2 stalks of celery, leaves included

1 medium apple, green, cored

½ cup baby spinach

Parsley (a few sprigs depending on your preference)

½ lemon

Directions:

1. Juice all the ingredients together for a creamy and fulfilling breakfast drink.

A Massive Green Breakfast

Serving Size: 7-8 ounces

Best Prepared With: Centrifugal Juicers

As far as breakfast juices go, this green breakfast probably comes closest to the perfect meal. The ingredients are well chosen and span a variety of fruits and vegetables to provide a satisfying and complete slate of nutritional goodness. Apples, carrots and cucumber form the base and accentuated by the addition of pepper for flavoring and an almost imperceptible kick.

In addition, the spinach provides the perfect dash of green goodness that's rich in disease fighting antioxidants. Spinach is also great for detoxifying because of its high fiber content. This is matched well by the inclusion of tomatoes, everyone's favorite salad-turned-juice ingredient. Topping everything off are grapes!

Now that's a breakfast that you can be proud of.

Ingredients:

2 medium apples, cored

3 medium carrots, peeled

1 small cucumber

90-grams of green grapes

1 small pepper, sweet green variety

1 cup spinach

1 medium tomato

Directions:

1. Process all ingredients and serve.

Afternoon Refreshments

If breakfast recipes are mainly defined by their "start-your-day-right" characteristics, afternoon juices tend to be more relaxed and laid back. Juices for this time of the day are intended to provide a refreshing and calming effect, the type of drink that you'd pine for while lounging poolside on a fine summer day.

But just because these recipes are laid-back does not mean you'd have to already give up on the "healthy" aspect. *Au contraire.*

Afternoon juices need to be refreshing but still filling because they should be able to tie your day together, bridging you from lunch to dinner. A perfectly crafted afternoon juice should be able to erase your hunger pangs so you are less likely to grab some unhealthy snacks from the office pantry.

Here are 7 juicing recipes that are perfect for your afternoon break.

Summertime Mojito

Serving Size: 1-2 ounces

Best Prepared With: Centrifugal Juicers

This is a light and easy recipe, one that packs "just enough" without being too much or too overwhelming. The cucumber is juicy and refreshing and the pear provides some volume and meat but otherwise, this drink reminds you of a mojito after a long and tiring day.

The smell of mint and the acidity from the lime spells the perfect relaxing vibe to a stressful day at the office.

Ingredients:

1 medium cucumber
1 medium pear
1 ½ cups of mint
½ lime

Directions:

1. Juice and serve.

Energize Me!

Serving Size: 3-4 ounces

Best Prepared With: Masticating or Triturating Juicers

If you're the type that dislikes big and heavy breakfasts and prefers heavy lunches instead, this is the recipe for you. Like the massive green breakfast but with a characteristic twist to suit lunch, this recipe features a boatload of ingredients that are specifically selected to provide you with a complete array of nutrients that should last you until the early evening.

The abundance of leafy greens also makes this juice a bit different from your typical juicing recipe. This produces a drink that is more smoothie than it is juice and is therefore important if you want a filling option for a mid-day binge. Try it out and see if this green wave of ingredients suits your taste.

Ingredients:

2 medium apples

½ cucumber

½ lemon, peeled

½ cup kale

½ cup spinach

¼ cup celery

¼ bulb fennel

1 thumb ginger

¼ of medium-sized romaine lettuce head

Directions:

1. Juice and stir together.

Carrot-Mango Supreme

Serving Size: 4-5 ounces

Best Prepared With: Centrifugal Juicers

Does this sound like an ice cream to you?

Well, the combination of carrots and mango which produces a thick, creamy liquid when blended for more than a few minutes gives this juice the illusion of being almost ice cream-like. And if that's not enough, consider how the orange peel and the addition of navel orange gives it another dimension, an almost subtle aftertaste that will bring you back for more.

If you are pining for a refreshing drink on a warm summer's day, you can never go wrong with the carrot-mango supreme.

Ingredients:

8 medium carrots

1 mango, pitted

1 large strip of orange peel

½ peeled navel orange

Crushed ice (optional)

Directions:

1. Juice and drink immediately. If you are using a blender, you can add the ice first before dropping in the other ingredients.

Tropicana Delight

Serving Size: 2-3 ounces

Best Prepared With: Centrifugal Juicers

The star in this recipe is the pineapple and it is certainly an ingredient that brings the idea of "Tropicana" to the fore. Pineapples are rich in antioxidants like beta carotene and are therefore awesome for weight loss. Pineapples are also refreshing particularly when eaten or juiced fresh instead of from a can.

In addition to the pineapples, the beets contribute their fair share of betalains that complement the beta carotene. The carrots also pack a lot of goodness as you may already know from previous recipes.

All told, this light and refreshing juice will leave you full and fresh right up to dinner.

Ingredients:

½ beet

2 medium carrots

1 stalk of celery, leaves included

½ medium cucumber

1 inch ginger

½ cup parsley

2 rounds pineapple

Directions:

1. Wash and juice together. Grate the ginger if you want a more eventually distributed kick to your Tropicana delight.

Simple-and-Svelte Carrot and Apple Juice

Serving Size: 3-4 ounces

Best Prepared With: Centrifugal Juicers

This recipe is perfect for the no-frills juicer who just wants a good drink with few complications. Carrots and apples are proven commodities in the juicing world.

They pack a lot of nutrients, are readily available, and require little preparation to be juiced. If you want a simple but svelte recipe that hits at all the right parts without keeping you in the kitchen for more than a few minutes, this is the recipe for you.

Ingredients:

4 medium carrots

1 medium apple, green, pitted

Directions:

1. Drop them in and enjoy the juice!

Afternoon Surprise

Serving Size: 1-2 ounces

Best Prepared With: Centrifugal Juicers

This recipe goes back to the idea that juicing need not be a complicated venture for anyone. In fact, at the core of juicing is the concept of being able to essentially pull out ingredients from your crisper, freezer, or countertop and to be able to make something healthy out of those ingredients.

Try the Afternoon Surprise and build from the simplicity of this recipe with the end goal of growing more comfortable with juicing ingredients for any meal of the day.

Ingredients:

1 stalk of celery

1 medium apple, cored

Directions:

1. Make sure to core the apples first before juicing them.

Pick-Me-Up Delight

Serving Size: 3-4 ounces

Best Prepared With: Centrifugal Juicers

The Pick-Me-Up Delight takes advantage of the complementary flavors of the tomato, orange, carrots and apple to create a recipe that is a bit whimsical but also equally practical. Carrots and apples tend to provide a hint of sweetness from the sugars while tomatoes and oranges give some much needed acidity and contrast to any dish.

The result of this combination is a potent wake-me-up drink that isn't only healthy but is also easily doable for anyone who wants to juice on a regular basis.

Ingredients:

1 medium tomato

1 large orange

2 large carrots

1 apple, Granny Smith preferred but not required, cored

Directions:

1. Juice the harder ingredients first, so start with the carrots working all the way down to the tomato. This will give your drink a layered and structured taste that works for any stressful afternoon, whether at home or at work.

Perfect For Dinner

Dinner juicing recipes often straddle the fine line between "filling" and refreshing depending on the juicer's preferences. Some juicers would prefer that their juices are full of fiber and can be made as a complete substitute for a solid meal; hence, volume becomes a major priority when making these juices.

On the other hand, there are juicers who want light beverages. The idea here is to simulate the concept of going "to the bar" after a long and stressful day and indulging on your favorite alcoholic drink to calm the nerves.

Unfortunately for us, alcohol isn't on the recommended shortlist for healthy ingredients when juicing for weight loss. Hence, it becomes imperative to find a suitable substitute without having to cross the line into actually drinking a cocktail or a much stronger drink.

In the following recipes, therefore, you will find a combined attempt to fulfill both the need to have drinks that are filling as well as drinks that are refreshing. Lemons and lime, that ever subtle reminder of cocktail drinks, is a rather common sight in many of these recipes.

Still, provided that you take your juicing, you can be confident that these recipes will pave the way to weight loss and better health.

End-of-Day Ensemble

Serving Size: 3-4 ounces

Best Prepared With: Centrifugal or Triturating Juicers

What constitutes the perfect end-of-day drink? How about an ensemble of many common ingredients which firmly puts you on track towards meeting your goal of a fulfilling but refreshing drink?

The heft and fullness in this end-of-day ensemble primarily comes from the beet, cucumber, carrot and apple and as you can see, there is no shortage of satisfying ingredients. The kale provides some added color and contrast to the recipe, leaving behind a sense of bitterness that negates the sweetness of the beets, carrots and apples. Tying it all together is the hint of lemon and lime that gives you the "refreshing" side of the recipe.

You can be confident this is the perfect recipe to kick off your juicing during dinner.

Ingredients:

1 beet, sliced
1 medium cucumber
1 medium carrot
1 medium apple, cored
4 leaves of kale
¼ lemon, peeled
¼ lime, peeled

Directions:

1. Juice everything as per the instructions in your specific juicer. Starting from soft towards the harder ingredients always works for me.

Weight Loss Watcher's Favorite

Serving Size: 5-6 ounces

Best Prepared With: Centrifugal Juicers

The Weight Loss Watcher's recipe excels in a few areas that help promote weight loss. First, its ingredients are specifically chosen for this purpose. Apples and carrots are very filling but also rich in natural sugars that help curb appetite. Cucumber provides plenty of water that aids in detoxification.

And the ginger, as usual, gives you the impression that you aren't drinking just any other healthy drink. Blend the ginger properly and you can be confident you'll have an interesting and playful drink that ticks all the right boxes in your weight loss checklist.

Guaranteed, this one will be one of your favorites in no time.

Ingredients:

5 carrots

1 red apple

1 small cucumber

1 beet, washed well, peeled, sliced

1 stalk of celery

1 thumb of ginger (optional)

Directions:

1. Grate the ginger first if you want a more even blending of the flavors.
2. Juice everything and enjoy a definite crowd favorite.

Grapefruits Galore

Serving Size: 3-4 ounces

Best Prepared With: Centrifugal Juicers

Grapefruits are distant relatives of the berry family and because of it, grapefruits are well-renowned for their high antioxidant content. We've already talked about antioxidants in detail; how it helps fight illnesses, strengthens the immune system, negates the effects of stress, and has anti-inflammatory properties among many other properties.

Try this recipe and enjoy the interesting flavors of a grapefruit-starred juice drink.

Ingredients:

2 grapefruits, peeled, pitted, chopped
5 carrots
1-inch ginger, peeled, chopped

Directions:

1. Press grapefruits, ginger, and carrots, together. Stir and serve.

Cranberry Craziness

Serving Size: 3-4 ounces

Best Prepared With: Centrifugal Juicers

Like grapefruits, cranberries benefit from its closeness to the berry family. In fact, cranberries are considered one of the most nutritious fruits in the world bordering on being classified as a superfood.

So what can a cranberry do for your weight loss goals? Well, there are many health benefits that can be ascribed to cranberries including lower bad cholesterol levels, prevention of kidney problems, and helping to stave off the effects of aging by virtue of its high antioxidant content.

Try this Cranberry Craziness and get hooked on the healthy goodness of cranberries.

Ingredients:

1 cup fresh cranberries (about 230 grams)

2 large oranges

5 carrots

Directions:

1. Juice the cranberries first so it serves as the base of the drink. Add the carrots and oranges as you normally would with any other recipe. Enjoy!

Sunset and Sexy

Serving Size: 5-6 ounces

Best Prepared With: Centrifugal Juicers

Sunset often conjures images of the "fun" and the "mysterious." As night falls, bars all around the world open to welcome adventurous souls in, waiting for the rave that's sure to follow.

This sunset and sexy recipe follows the same mold in that it features a little bit of everything. The sweet potato is definitely a first in this recipe list but it works if you are able to juice it properly. The bell peppers are also interesting additions, bringing color and spice to the equation without being too overpowering and dominating on your palate.

The carrots, apples and oranges round up the group – a rather common and recurring sight but one that you'd definitely want to have in an after-dinner drink towards weight loss.

Ingredients:

1 large sweet potato

1 medium carrot

1 red bell pepper

2 large beets

2 apples

1 orange (optional)

Directions:

1. Wash and peel the sweet potato. Chop into small chunks and juice slow, a few pieces at a time.
2. Juice the other ingredients as you would in any other recipe.
3. Mix properly before serving.

Sour-and-Sweet and Oh-So-Great

Serving Size: 3-4 ounces

Best Prepared With: Centrifugal Juicers

The sweet-and-sour play on flavors is a time-honored tradition that is well reflected in many culinary masterpieces all over the world. For some reason, sour and sweet go really well together satisfying both your sweet-tooth cravings and your adult penchant for acidity in one serving.

This recipe takes that same concept and deftly applies it to juicing. The beet, carrots and apple provide the sweet flavor while the grapefruit sprinkles in a dash of the sour. Add in the ginger and you know you're just an alcohol drop away from a real party.

Ingredients:

1 apple
4 large carrots
1 beet

1 inch ginger

1-2 cups grapefruit

Directions:

1. Grate the ginger and juice all the other ingredients. Mix and serve.

Extra-Veggie Extravaganza

Serving Size: 10-12 ounces

Best Prepared With: Triturating Juicers

This recipe is a no-holds-barred take on healthy juicing. It's a lot to take but it works quite well with people who want to fully do away with dinner without having to wake up in the middle of night and craving for a midnight snack.

In addition, this recipe is designed such that the resulting drink preserves well in the refrigerator so you can enjoy a second serving the day after. If you are eyeing to prepare one drink that lasts you two days or so, this extra-veggie extravaganza is extraordinarily suited for your extra day goals.

Ingredients:

3 medium tomatoes, cut into chunks
7 stalks of celery stalks
½ pound carrots

1 medium horseradish, peeled

¼ teaspoon salt

2 ½ teaspoons lemon juice, freshly squeezed

Directions:

1. Blend or juice all the ingredients. Store in a big flask or pitcher. The drink can last up to two days.

Make use of these recipes by checking out the weight loss plan below.

The 14-Day Juicing Plan

So now we have the recipes; how do we put together a working juicing plan? Well, we didn't say juicing was easy if we didn't truly mean it. Below is a very simple table that you can actually print and stick on your refrigerator door.

Day	Breakfast	Afternoon	Dinner
1	Green Goblet of Goodness	Energize Me!	Grapefruits Galore
2	Ginger Ale	Carrot-Mango Supreme	Sunset and Sexy
3	Beet and Apple Juice	Pick-Me-Up Delight	End-of-Day Ensemble
4	Juicy Jolt	Simple-and-Svelte Carrot and Apple Juice	Sour-and-Sweet and Oh-So-Great
5	Filler-Upper	Afternoon Surprise	Weight Loss Watcher's

			Favorite
6	Carrot Care	Tropicana Delight	Cranberry Craziness
7	Massive Green Breakfast	Summer Mojito	Extra-Veggie Extravaganza
8	Beet and Apple Juice	Energize Me!	Extra-Veggie Extravaganza
9	Filler-Upper	Simple-and-Svelte Carrot and Apple Juice	Sunset and Sexy
10	Juicy Jolt	Pick-Me-Up Delight	Cranberry Craziness
11	Green Goblet of Goodness	Afternoon Surprise	End-of-Day Ensemble
12	Massive Green Breakfast	Summer Mojito	Grapefruits Galore
13	Ginger Ale	Carrot-Mango Supreme	Sour-and-Sweet and Oh-So-Great

| 14 | Carrot Care | Tropicana Delight | Weight Loss Watcher's Favorite |

How To Use This Plan

1. You can follow this plan for the next 14 days using one juicing recipe each for breakfast, afternoon snack, and dinner as outlined in the table below. This is specifically designed such that you'd never get bored of the recipes, you always get a new taste each and every day for the next 14 days, and that the serving sizes are balanced out so you more-or-less get the same nutritional benefits throughout all the 14 days.

2. I often recommend starting the juicing plan on a weekend. Many of us have a penchant for starting things out on a Monday because it is the beginning of the week but this can create havoc on your, your schedule, your routines, and your body in general. By starting on the weekend, you can have some time to adjust to the effects of juicing.

3. Before jumping right into the plan, go back and read the section on preparing yourself. Make sure you take the time to assess your situation and your readiness before committing to the plan. This is not a passing fad; take it seriously and it can produce great results that will change the way you view your health.

4. One question: With this plan, does it mean I can already completely skip my meals for the next 14 days? That's a tough question to answer because every juicer differs ever so slightly that there are no universal answers that applies to everyone. In a nutshell, this plan is designed so you can comfortably live off of the plan without needing meals. However, if you feel you are not ready for this, you can always make the personal decision to either cut one or two meals from your day leaving you with just 1 meal, for example, and 3 juicing recipes for the whole day.

5. If you choose to follow the plan without any solid meals, I recommend that you evaluate your hunger and cravings based on the first few days of the plan. If necessary, prepare more of the juice and drink more servings throughout the day. I also recommend that you consider adding honey or molasses into certain recipes so you can have a quick infusion of sugars and calories to fuel you throughout the work day. It will take some getting used to but I guarantee, it will produce results that will blow you away.

6. On shopping for ingredients, think about the schedule that works for you. For this juicing plan, I recommend shopping twice a week. Get your ingredients for the next 3 days but don't buy everything to prevent wastage. Even the best storage plans can run into ruin just because a few factors like the weather or the freshness of the ingredient is already out-of-whack right at the onset.

Good luck and may you enjoy your decision to commit to a healthier lifestyle.

Conclusion

I've said more than enough in these last few pages and I'm sure you have a lot of information to take on. Just allow me to reiterate a few salient points that are important towards enjoying juicing as a lifestyle and for producing impressive weight loss results.

1. Juicing is very simple and easy to do. The secret is in committing to try it for a few days, see for yourself the results that it produces, and from there judging whether it is the best plan for your health and weight.

2. Always buy the freshest ingredients. The ingredients that you juice are at the core of whether or not you get good results.

3. Experiment and enjoy. There is no universal rule to juicing. If you want to try out an ingredient, go ahead and do so. There is no

juicing police that prevents you from doing things provided you are doing them correctly.

4. Juicing takes time to master. Your body also needs time to adapt. However, if you put in the commitment, you should be a master juicer in virtually no time at all.

5. Talk to your doctor about juicing and how it can benefit you. It is always best to check with the professionals so you are given the best advice that suits your specific situation.

Best of luck on your juicing journey!

Enjoy this book?

Please leave a review below and let us know what you liked about this book by clicking on the Amazon image below.

and click on Digital Orders.

The above link directs to Amazon.com. Please change the .com to your own country extension.

Made in United States
Orlando, FL
10 April 2023

31945554R00074